Edited by
ANDREW ROBERTS
NEIL JOHNSON
and **TOM MILTON**

FELLOWSHIP

66 They devoted themselves
to the apostles' teaching and to
fellowship, to the breaking 99
of bread and to prayer.

The Bible Reading Fellowship
15 The Chambers, Vineyard
Abingdon OX14 3FE
brf.org.uk

The Bible Reading Fellowship (BRF) is a Registered Charity (233280)

ISBN 978 0 85746 679 2
First published 2018
10 9 8 7 6 5 4 3 2 1 0
All rights reserved

Text © individual authors 2018
This edition © The Bible Reading Fellowship 2018
Original design by morsebrowndesign.co.uk & penguinboy.net

The authors assert the moral right to be identified as the authors of this work

Acknowledgements

Unless otherwise acknowledged, scripture quotations from The New Revised Standard Version of the Bible, Anglicised edition, copyright © 1989, 1995 by the Division of Christian Education of the National Council of the churches of Christ in the United States of America. Used by permission. All rights reserved.

Scripture quotations on cover and title page are taken from The Holy Bible, New International Version (Anglicised edition) copyright © 1979, 1984, 2011 by Biblica. Used by permission of Hodder & Stoughton Publishers, a Hachette UK company. All rights reserved. 'NIV' is a registered trademark of Biblica. UK trademark number 1448790.

Extracts from the Authorised Version of the Bible (The King James Bible), the rights in which are vested in the Crown, are reproduced by permission of the Crown's Patentee, Cambridge University Press.

Photograph on page 11 copyright © Thinkstock; photographs on pages 29, 31, 42 and 62 copyright © Tom Milton and the Birmingham Methodist Circuit; photograph on page 4 copyright © Aike Kennett-Brown; photograph on page 38 by Rebecca J Hall; photograph on page 40 copyright © Marty Woods.

Every effort has been made to trace and contact copyright owners for material used in this resource. We apologise for any inadvertent omissions or errors, and would ask those concerned to contact us so that full acknowledgement can be made in the future.

A catalogue record for this book is available from the British Library

Printed and bound by CPI Group (UK) Ltd, Croydon CR0 4YY

CONTENTS

Remember the context

This Holy Habit is set in the context of ten Holy Habits, and the ongoing life of your church and community.

> **They devoted themselves to** the apostles' teaching and **fellowship**, to the breaking of bread and the prayers. Awe came upon everyone, because many wonders and signs were being done by the apostles. All who believed were together and had all things in common; they would sell their possessions and goods and distribute the proceeds to all, as any had need. Day by day, as they spent much time together in the temple, they broke bread at home and ate their food with glad and generous hearts, praising God and having the goodwill of all the people. And day by day the Lord added to their number those who were being saved.
>
> ACTS 2:42–47

A prayer for the faithful practice of Holy Habits

This prayer starts with a passage from Romans 5:4–5.

Endurance produces character, and character produces hope,
    and hope does not disappoint us…
Gracious and ever-loving God, we offer our lives to you.
Help us always to be open to your Spirit in our thoughts
    and feelings and actions.
Support us as we seek to learn more about those habits of the Christian life
    which, as we practise them, will form in us the character of Jesus
    by establishing us in the way of faith, hope and love.
Amen

INTRODUCTION

The Greek word translated as **Fellowship** in Acts 2 is *koinonia*. It is a word rich in depth, meaning and challenge. It points to a quality of relationship and activity which is so much deeper than the chit-chat over a tepid cup of tea and a soggy digestive that sadly sometimes passes for **Fellowship**.

Koinonia is profoundly practical and deeply relational. John Stott argues that *koinonia* 'is a Trinitarian experience, it is our common share in God, Father, Son and Holy Spirit' (*The Message of Acts*, Inter-Varsity Press, 1990, p. 83). In Acts 2, *koinonia* is seen in followers of Jesus eating, praying and sharing goods together. In short, sharing their lives with each other and the world around them, in a prophetic symbol of the kingdom of God: a powerful sign of a Spirit-filled way of life that stands against sinful selfishness; a wonder of hope, reconciliation and generosity; a true community of belonging and service. Through the practical expression of Christ-like love, *koinonia* draws people to Jesus, nurturing and sustaining disciples. It is evangelistic (good news), pastoral, practical and formative.

There is a risk that in deepening **Fellowship**, Christians can become insular. So, as you explore this habit, let us keep asking how can we, personally and collectively, practise this habit beyond the **Fellowship** of the gathered church, in our places of work, in the community and especially with those who suffer or are disconnected?

 Resources particularly suitable for children and families

 Resources particularly suitable for young people

CH4 Church Hymnary 4 (also known as Hymns of Glory Songs of Praise)
RS   Rejoice and Sing
SoF Songs of Fellowship 6
StF Singing the Faith

Reflections

Fellowship invokes images of close, supportive, personal relationships, including: small groups of mutual care and sharing and times of prayer, study and conversation with fellow Christians, as well as being nurtured in our spiritual lives through the encouragement and companionship of our friends in the Christian community. These are powerful expressions of **Fellowship** to be celebrated, nurtured and encouraged, reminding us of our need to draw alongside one another prayerfully and supportively on our faith journey.

Our Christian faith is not simply a private, personal affair; it unites us to one another through Christ and is at its most enriching and life-giving when experienced in **Fellowship** and community with each other and with God. 'Where two or three are gathered together in my name, there am I in the midst of them' (Matthew 18:20, KJV). But we must be careful not to confuse **Fellowship** with closed groups which have formed such strong relationships and bonds that it is very difficult for others to be welcomed and embraced within them. **Fellowship**/*koinonia* by its very definition is a celebration both of loving gracious relationships and of open-heartedness towards others.

A church in the Birmingham Methodist Circuit, which first developed these resources, was blessed by the joy and challenge of welcoming a young couple seeking asylum. They enriched the **Fellowship** which the members of the church shared, and connected them with diverse experiences of another culture which has a particular emphasis on hospitality, caring and generosity of spirit, despite the hostility they have faced.

As you ponder **Fellowship**, reflect upon the ways in which you practise *koinonia* in your church and small groups. Give thanks for and celebrate those expressions of relationship with God and each other. Consider prayerfully and honestly how we sometimes fall short of the glory of God by neglecting our need for Christian **Fellowship**. How far does our **Fellowship** echo the self-giving gracious nature of our Trinitarian God's relationship with us and all?

UNDERSTANDING THE HABIT

WORSHIP RESOURCES

Below are some thoughts and ideas for how you might incorporate this Holy Habit into worship.

Biblical material

Old Testament passages:

- Genesis 18:1–16   Abraham offers hospitality to three visitors
- Psalm 111   Worship in **Fellowship** with God and each other

Gospel passages:

- Matthew 18:15–20   Restoring community and overcoming divisions
- Luke 19:1–10   Zacchaeus
- John 15:1–17   Jesus, the true vine
- John 17:6–26   The prayer of Jesus that the church may be one

Other New Testament passages:

- 1 Corinthians 3:1–11   Paul and Apollos
- 1 Corinthians 10:17–22   Though we are many, we are one body
- 2 Corinthians 13:11–13   The grace
- Galatians 2:1–10   Paul and the other apostles
- Galatians 3:23–29   Divided no more; all one in Christ
- Philippians 2:1–16   United in purpose and serving alongside one another
- 1 John 1:1–7   Fellowship with Christ

Suggested hymns and songs

- All praise to our redeeming Lord (HP 753, StF 608)
- Bless and keep us, Lord (RS 471)
- Brother, sister, let me serve you (CH4 694, RS 474, StF 611)
- Christ for the world we sing (RS 561)
- Christ, from whom all blessings flow (RS 561, StF 676)
- Colours of day dawn into the mind (RS 572, StF 167) 🚹🚹
- He's got the whole world in his hand (StF 536) 🚹🚹
- I come with joy, a child of God (CH4 656, RS 447, StF 588)
- In Christ there is no east or west (CH4 624, RS 647, StF 685)
- Jesus calls us here to meet him (RS 510, StF 28)
- Jesus, Lord, we look to thee (RS 564, StF 686)
- Let us build a house (All are welcome) (CH4 198, StF 409)
- Lord we remember your people (RS 754)
- Summoned by the God who made us (StF 689)
- Thanks for friends who keep on loving (StF 619)
- The church is like a table (RS 480)
- The church is wherever God's people (CH4 522, RS 583)
- There's a wideness in God's mercy (CH4 187, RS 353, StF 416)

Introduction to the theme 👨‍👩‍👧‍👦

Luke 19:1–10

Retell the story of Zacchaeus being restored to **Fellowship**, using your preferred translation of the Bible (consider a children's Bible), or show a video clip such as the 'Brick Bible' version (**youtu.be/DdOSWhqQwhw**, or search YouTube for 'Brick Bible Zacchaeus').

- At the start of the story, we see Zacchaeus is alone and has no friends. How do you think he feels about having no friends?
- Does the story have a happy ending?
- Why does the story end on a positive note?

Because Zacchaeus returns the money he has wrongly taken, we assume he is welcomed back by his neighbours. He can be friends with people again because Jesus has shown what it means to be a true friend.

Today, we are thinking about the Holy Habit of **Fellowship**.

Let's look up the dictionary definition of the word '**Fellowship**'. (Find a suitable volunteer to look up the word in a paper or electronic dictionary. The definition should read something like this: **Fellowship** is friendship or companionship based on shared interests or a shared aim.)

So, let's think again about the story of Zacchaeus.

Consider the things that are good examples of **Fellowship** within the story and the things that are not good examples of **Fellowship**.

I am going to read out some statements about the story of Zacchaeus. If you think that the statement shows a good example of **Fellowship**, give a thumbs-up sign and I will put that statement in the red box/bucket/bag. If you think that the statement does NOT show a good example of **Fellowship**, put your thumbs down and I will put that statement in the yellow box/bucket/bag. (In a church with digital projection facilities, an electronic version of this activity could be devised.)

Good examples of fellowship
- Jesus goes to Zacchaeus' house for a meal
- Zacchaeus is honest about the wrong way he has treated people
- Zacchaeus returns the money
- Zacchaeus is seen as a 'Son of Abraham', not as an outsider.

Not good examples of fellowship
- Zacchaeus is alone in the crowd
- Zacchaeus tries to get above everyone else so that he can listen to Jesus
- Zacchaeus is greedy and dishonest by taking other people's money.

Message
The Bible includes stories where Jesus meets characters like Zacchaeus, whom no one wanted to be friends with, where Jesus brings the person into **Fellowship** with God and with people around them. It is easy for us to have **Fellowship** and be friends with people we like but Jesus encourages us also to have **Fellowship** with people we don't like as much. We need to ask for God's help to start such friendships and to keep them going when life is difficult as well as when life is happy.

Prayer

Lord Jesus, thank you for being our friend. Help us to be good friends to others and to live in fellowship. Teach us to respect others, to listen to them and work together in the ways of justice and peace.
Amen

Thoughts for sermon preparation

Galatians 2:1–10; 2 Corinthians 13:13

There are several references to **Fellowship**/*koinonia* in the New Testament which provide opportunities for preaching on **Fellowship**. In Galatians 2:9, Paul records how James, Cephas (Peter) and John gave to Barnabas and Paul himself 'the right hand of fellowship'. This term and form of greeting and welcome are used in services such as admission to membership and confirmation services. It is a sign of belonging to the church of Christ, just as it was for Paul and Barnabas in the first century. It did not lead to withdrawing from the world into tight-knit Christian communal living, but to going out into the world and sharing in God's mission. The sharing of the 'right hand of fellowship' leads to an affirmation of Peter's ministry amongst the Jews, the circumcised, and Paul's sending out to the uncircumcised, the Gentiles. **Fellowship**/*koinonia* is the springboard to mission, breaking through these boundaries and looking outward to new relationships.

This passage is also in the context of the collection for Christians in Jerusalem. Paul concludes in verse 10, 'They asked only one thing, that we remember the poor, which was actually what I was keen to do.' Whenever Paul urged the church to remember the poor in Jerusalem, he spoke of the unity that all Christians have in Christ. To that he added the importance of responding to those who are suffering because we are inextricably related to one another through our relationship with God. We are one in the body of Christ and we are each a part.

In a more recent example, Methodist churches are joined together in what is known as the 'Connexion'. This was built on a theology of individuals' deep connectedness with one another through connection in Christ. Again, this was not intended as a call to an impenetrable holy huddle, but sought and served to shape faith outwards toward the world and a wider vision of Christian communion beyond the local.

In 2 Corinthians 13:13, Paul concludes his letter with a prayer that has often been used at the climax of our communal worship and meeting together: 'The grace of the Lord Jesus Christ, the love of God, and the communion [fellowship] of the Holy Spirit be with all of you.' Again, the word used is *koinonia*, expressed in terms of the **Fellowship** that we have with each other through the one Holy Spirit with which we have been blessed. It is a reminder that any **Fellowship** we have with each other is inspired first by the gracious relationship we have with God, through our Lord Jesus Christ. Given the divisions that Paul was urging the church in Corinth to overcome, these final words take on an even greater power, urging the Christian community there to live in unity, remembering primarily the grace and love of God for all.

Two millennia on, the Christian church still struggles and wrestles with what it means to be one in the Holy Spirit through God's love and the grace of Christ. We struggle to receive the gift of one church with one Lord and one faith. There are divisions in our own churches, and divisions between Christian denominations. When speaking these words through a comforting smile, they trip off our tongue comfortably. Embracing relationships of radical love and grace in Christ and towards all God's people is rather more challenging.

Prayers

A call to worship

Heavenly Father,
in this celebration of the Holy Habits
we are called to be in fellowship with one another,
a true and loving togetherness that
can only come from a communion with you,
and a love for all those around us.

Today, we come together to learn and experience
the true meaning of fellowship on life's journey.
Open our hearts to your word, we pray.
Amen

A call to worship

Based on 1 Corinthians 1:9.

Faithful God,
You have called us as your people into fellowship with you,
through Your Son, Jesus Christ, our Lord and Saviour.

We come humbly before you this day;
may our hearts and minds be open to your Word,
as we share together in worship,
through the fellowship of the Holy Spirit.
Amen

A prayer of praise, adoration and confession

Gracious God,
you have brought us here together today because you love us.
In response to that overpowering and unconditional love,
we join to worship and adore you.
We have come from different backgrounds and different places,
yet we are one in praise for you.

You brought the universe, in all its wonder, into being.
Your love is beyond compare,
and yet you know each one of us,
and call us by name.
How wonderful!

Connected by this fellowship with you and one another,
we share in the ups and downs of life,
experiencing joys and sorrows together.
We support and guide,
through the power of your Holy Spirit,
and in your name we bring our prayers of praise today.

But we know only too well
that this fellowship with you and one another
is not a closed order.
Your welcome and your love is for all,
but we have to confess that we are not always welcoming,
as that takes effort and time.
We can be so preoccupied with comfort,
or with people we know,
that we do not welcome the stranger.
We don't reach out to touch and embrace a newcomer.

We know our failings, and do little to make a difference.
Forgive us.

(*Silence*)

Encourage us, Lord, to look outside our comfortable circles,
and be ready with arms outstretched to welcome in your name.
By your grace, we receive your forgiveness,
and strive to make a difference.
Amen

A prayer of intercession

In **Fellowship** together, we turn again to prayer.

Gentle Lord, you gave us hands, that we might hold another. Hands that can shake, grasp and carry. May our touch be always tender and loving. We remember those who face real cruelty at the hands of others, and try to understand their fears. We are reminded that our names are printed on the palms of your hands, a fact that we need to highlight and share, in love.

Lord, together we turn to you
and turn outwards to embrace the world

Loving Lord, you gave us arms to embrace, to give strength to others. Arms that will lift, welcome and direct. We long to use all that we have and are, to work for you in love. We are very aware of arms that hurt and abuse, where love is lacking or absent, arms that bring sadness, and we pray for those who suffer the pain of not feeling loved.

We ask that we may have arms of reconciliation and forgiveness for those who cause war or conflict. For those involved in trying to resolve conflict, we pray that they may have courage, wisdom and humanity. For those caught up in war and conflict, we ask for peace, real peace.

Lord, together we turn to you
and turn outwards to embrace the world.

Caring Lord, you gave us feet to walk in your footsteps, to serve and work for you. Help us to encourage others to join us on our journey, encompassing with care and hospitality. At the same time, we remember those who struggle in life's journey, who feel they have lost their way, as well as those whose feet are no longer fit to make the physical journey to be with their congregations. Use our feet to visit, prayerfully, lest they feel forgotten.

As refugees in a strange land, many are walking without direction. Encourage us as we invite them to join us in fellowship.

Lord, together we turn to you
and turn outwards to embrace the world.
Amen

A prayer of thanksgiving

Gracious God,
Thank you that you have called us to live in fellowship
with you and with others.

Thank you for the good things that we receive
by being part of communities
both within and outside the church.

Thank you for your infinite patience with us
when we fall short in our response
to the fellowship which you offer us.
Thank you.
Amen

A prayer of blessing

May God the Father keep us in communion with him,
May God the Son lead us in his footsteps and
May God the Holy Spirit encourage us to embrace all,
connecting with those we know, and those we don't,
in true communion love, and may we leave in peace and thankfulness.
Amen

A prayer for those out of fellowship

After each sentence, pause to allow people to pray quietly for those who come to mind.

Gracious God.
We pray for those who find themselves alone, who long for companionship.

We pray for those forbidden to meet with brothers and sisters in Christ,
or denied the opportunity to do so.

We pray for those who have walked away from Christian communities
that have loved them and still pray for them.

We pray for those who have been hurt or abused
in the name of fellowship.

We pray for those who no longer feel welcome or loved
in a fellowship they once held dear.

We pray for fellowships where the flame of the Spirit
seems to have been extinguished.

Gracious God, Father, Son and Holy Spirit who dwell in community,
restore, renew and heal those we remember in prayer today.
May the grace of our Lord Jesus Christ,
the love of God
and the fellowship of the Holy Spirit
be more than words for them and us.
May they be reality restored.
Amen

Different ways of praying

Prayers for others

Invite the congregation to say one-sentence prayers for people, places or situations about which they are concerned. After each prayer use the bidding, 'And all the people said…'

The congregation should respond, 'Amen'.

Remember to teach the response before you begin.

Prayers of blessing

Write a selection of blessings on bookmarks or pieces of paper. At the end of your service (e.g. during the last hymn or song), hand them around the congregation.

Invite people to say the blessing to their neighbour and then give it to them.

Encourage them to pass the piece of paper on to a family member, friend or neighbour.

On future occasions, provide blank bookmarks and invite people to write their own blessings.

Woven prayers

Provide long strips of coloured paper or ribbons and invite participants to write or draw prayers on the strips, praying as they think and write. Make clear that the strips will be shared, so that people can share (or not) appropriately – for example, a face might be drawn rather than a name written.

When individual prayers are written, the strips are woven together at right angles to each other – alternating over and under in each direction to form a woven sheet.

Draw the prayer time to a close with an explanation that the weaving together represents the **Fellowship** of the body of Christ in prayer supporting each other as one, a physical expression of holding our prayers 'in common' as in Acts 2.

Ball of wool prayer

You will need a large ball of wool.

Start by holding on to the end of the wool and then unwinding it as you pass it to someone else (but keep hold of the end!). The next person holds the ball of wool. At this point you could ask them to introduce themselves, or to say something that they are thankful for, or you may choose not to ask them to say anything at all at this point.

The ball of wool continues to be unwound and passed on, with the next person keeping hold of the wool and so on. It is more effective if the wool is not passed to the person next to you, but to someone on the other side of the circle or church.

Eventually, as the ball of wool gets passed around, it creates a spider's web effect with everyone connected.

At this point, you could pray in a number of different ways using the wool. You could ask everyone to pray for the people whom they are directly connected to via the piece of wool, i.e. the person who passed it to them, and the person they passed it on to.

Alternatively, you could cut the wool, so that everyone now has a small piece of wool. Encourage people to keep this piece of wool and tie it somewhere where they will see it to remind them to pray for all those that were connected, and to be thankful for the **Fellowship** that they have with those people.

Gingerbread hearts prayer

Give each person a gingerbread person, available in boxes from many major supermarkets (or make your own).

Using a bag of icing, or a tube of ready-made icing, invite people to pipe a heart on the gingerbread and, as they do so, to think about the people who are special in their lives.

Then invite everyone to hold their gingerbread person in their hands and ask God to hold each of the people they have named safe in his hands.

The Messy Church grace 👪

A prayer with actions, used with the kind permission of The Bible Reading Fellowship.

> The grace of our Lord Jesus Christ (*hands out in front, palms up*)
> The love of God (*hug yourself*)
> And the fellowship of the Holy Spirit (*hold hands in big circle*)
> Be with us all now and for ever (*still holding hands – throw arms in air*)
> Amen

Neighbours 👪

Give people a large sheet of paper. Ask them to draw their home in the centre and then draw stick people to represent their household.

Then add:

- houses and people they know who are their neighbours
- friends and their houses
- relatives and their houses
- schools and friends
- local shops and workers
- dance classes, clubs, uniformed organisations, etc.

Continue until the sheet is full of drawings of places and stick people, people's communities, everyone they come into contact with.

A prayer could be said or written and placed on it, thanking God for all the people in their lives. Ask God to look after all the people, praising God for all the plans he has for them and thanking him for all the people he has yet to bring into their lives.

Some of these small group materials are traditional Bible studies, some are more diverse session plans and others are short activities, reflections and discussions. Please choose materials appropriate to whatever group you are working with.

Koinonia ☺

Acts 2:42 and other verses

Discuss what the group think the word '**Fellowship**' means, and possibly mind map on a large sheet of paper. Perhaps use questions such as: What is **Fellowship**? What does **Fellowship** look like/feel like? Are you in **Fellowship** with anyone?

Explain that the Greek word in the original text is *koinonia*, which appears 20 times in the New Testament, the first in Acts 2:42.

Share the meaning of *koinonia*: **Fellowship**, sharing in common, communion. Christian **Fellowship** is a key aspect of Christian life. Believers in Christ are to come together in love, faith, and encouragement. It involves a willingness to share life in depth. That is the essence of *koinonia*. In a world where people are often self-centred, it is deeply countercultural – a prophetic symbol of the kingdom of God.

Look at *koinonia* through what it means to be with 'one another'. Discuss and/or mind map how you should behave around one another and treat one another.

Further study
Look at some of the following texts about being with one another and discuss what is happening in the text, how it relates to our lives, how we feel about what it is telling us to do. If possible, look at the same text in different versions of the Bible to see what the impact on meaning is (for example THE MESSAGE, The Word on the Street, NRSV).

A powerful example of what *koinonia* should look like can be found in a study of the phrase 'one another' in the Bible. Scripture commands us to:

- be devoted to one another (Romans 12:10)
- honour one another (Romans 12:10)
- live in harmony with one another (Romans 12:16; 1 Peter 3:8)
- accept one another (Romans 15:7)
- serve one another in love (Galatians 5:13)
- be kind and compassionate to one another (Ephesians 4:32)
- admonish one another (Colossians 3:16)
- encourage one another (1 Thessalonians 5:11; Hebrews 3:13)
- spur one another on toward love and good deeds (Hebrews 10:24)
- offer hospitality (1 Peter 4:9)
- love one another (1 Peter 1:22; 1 John 3:11, 23; 4:7, 11–12)

That is what true biblical *koinonia* should look like.

Resources based on this exploration of 'one another' can be found later on in this booklet.

Final prayers
Sit in a circle. With one person starting, each person prays for the person on their left. Move around the circle until everyone has been prayed for. Give the option of praying aloud or in silence – if praying in silence, people will need to say 'Amen' at the end of their prayer.

Entertaining angels

Genesis 18:1–16

Read the passage and explore these questions:

- What are your first thoughts on reading this passage?
- What questions do you have?

It would be an insult to the community if hospitality was not offered. Certain acts like washing of feet were a sign of acceptance of people at face value. Rest and relaxation would be part of the hospitality along with a meal. On leave taking, there should be peace between host and visitor.

1 Who are these three visitors?
2 How does Abraham show hospitality?
3 How can we as a church or as individuals do the same?

4 How does Abraham serve the visitors with love?
5 How can we serve others within and outside the church?
6 How does Abraham show acceptance?
7 How easy is it for us to show acceptance and why might it be important to do so?
8 Is it significant that in verse 13 the voice becomes that of 'the Lord' and what does this say to us?
9 Hebrews 13:2 says, 'Do not neglect to show hospitality to strangers, for by doing that some have entertained angels without knowing it.' How could this verse help us to think about **Fellowship** in a different way?

The idea of **Fellowship** with God is also an important one. In Philippians 3:10, Paul says: 'I want to know Christ and the power of his resurrection and the sharing of his sufferings by becoming like him in his death.'

In 2 Corinthians 13:13, Paul also prays that we have **Fellowship** with the Holy Spirit – something we regularly say in the words of the 'Grace'. How then do we see our **Fellowship** with God? What does it entail and why is it important?

In the icon by Andrei Rublev, known as *The Hospitality of Abraham* and also as *The Trinity* (find it online), we have an idea of what **Fellowship** with God might be. The picture shows the three angels who visited Abraham, but is also full of symbolism, often interpreted as the Trinity. Around the head of each figure is a circle of light or halo, to show holiness. As you draw your gaze further out from the picture, you see that, in relation to each other, the figures also form a circle. However, the circle is not complete, for there is a space at the table which draws the onlooker in. There is also a place at the table for those outside this group. What is also clear is that, while the figures have a relationship together, they are sitting in such a way that they also look outward, so they have communion with each other and with those beyond them.

1 How might this picture help us to understand **Fellowship** with God both for Abraham and ourselves?
2 What other things would you say were useful to help explain **Fellowship** with God?
3 What personal examples or anecdotes might you be willing to share to illustrate your **Fellowship** with God?
4 The figures in the icon look outward. What can we do to try to extend our hospitality, service and acceptance both within and beyond our church?
5 Spend some time in silent reflection thinking about what it means to be in **Fellowship** with one another and with God. Is God calling you to change?

Beyond friendship: Are fellowship and friendship the same? ☺

John 15:1–17

Begin by brainstorming the key elements of a good friendship. Either as a whole group or in pairs, write a definition of friendship.

Write or type out the statements below on to separate pieces of card (or, if you prefer, you could do this activity by just reading out the statements). Ask the group to pick up a card, read the statement and decide which of two piles to put it into: 'being a friend' or 'not being a friend'.

- They talk about themselves, but rarely ask about you and your life.
- They follow you on Facebook but you haven't actually seen or spoken to them in five years.
- They have borrowed money from you but never repaid it.
- They have told you that you dress badly.
- They gossip about you with other people.
- They criticise your choice of boyfriend/girlfriend/partner and try and split you up.
- They start a new job/course/relationship and spend less time with you.
- They tell you that you eat/drink too much and that you should cut back.
- You have argued with them and they say they can't forgive you.
- They don't have the same beliefs as you and so they try to change your opinions.
- They don't stand up for you when you are treated badly by others.
- They get you into trouble with the police.

Explore the following questions with the group:

- How important is it that friends have the same beliefs or lifestyle as you? Does that help to make the friendship closer and stronger?
- Are there differences in belief that would make a friendship impossible?
- Would you ever use the word **Fellowship** to describe the kind of friendship you have with your friends? Why, or why not?
- Would you move any of the statements above if the two piles were labelled 'being in **Fellowship**' and 'not being in **Fellowship**' instead?

Ask each member of the group to draw a target board (like one in archery) on to a piece of paper. Ask each person to write the names of their friends on the target board, with those friends that they are closest to written closer to the centre and those they are less close to written further out.

Explore where they may have put 'Facebook friends' on their target board – which circles did they fall into? Are Facebook friends 'real' friends? What makes them so, or not?

- Has anyone put Jesus on their target board?
- Think about the friends that you have in your church or faith groups. Would you ever use the word **Fellowship** to describe the kind of friendship you have with them? Why, or why not?
- Are there people in those groups who you consider are 'in **Fellowship**' with you but who you would not call friends?

Explore what people would be willing to do for each of their circles of friends by reading out the following statements and allowing people the opportunity to say whether they would do that for all their friends or just those in the closest circle(s). Encourage people not to use names at this point, especially if they are known to other people in the group.

Which of your friends would you:

- lend money to?
- give a gift to?
- invite to your house?
- go away on holiday with?
- offer advice to?
- stand up for and risk suffering for yourself?
- give up your life for?

Read John 15:9–17. You may find it helpful to explore the following questions in pairs first, before feeding back and discussing with the whole group.

- How does it feel to know that Jesus regards us as friends?
- What is Jesus prepared to do for his friends?
- Does knowing and accepting this change anything about your relationship with Jesus?
- Would you use the word '**Fellowship**' to describe your friendship with Jesus? Why, or why not?

Discuss together whether you can have **Fellowship** with someone you are not friends with. You might find it beneficial to read together the introduction and reflections at the beginning of this booklet to help you understand the meaning of **Fellowship**.

- How is **Fellowship** similar to the earlier definition of friendship you created?
- How is it different?

Close in personal reflective prayer, with each person reflecting upon their friendship with Jesus and whether they are in **Fellowship** with Jesus. You also may like to spend some time praying for the needs of friends. Pray too for the deepening of **Fellowship** between members of your group and the wider church and community.

Jelly activity 👪

You will need to prepare a bowl of jelly and attach two spoons to long poles or garden canes. You may need to put a cloth down if the front of the church is carpeted.

Invite two people to come and eat the jelly. The catch is that they can only hold their spoon at the far end of the cane.

When that proves impossible, invite them and other people present to think about how they might be able to eat the jelly.

When someone suggests that they feed each other (prompt them if not), invite them to try this so they can enjoy a spoonful of jelly.

After the food has been shared, suggest that this is an example of how we are to share together in Christian **Fellowship**: not looking out for ourselves, but looking outwards to others and sharing what we have.

Game of fellowship 👪

Divide people into two or three teams. Each team divides into two groups, who stand at opposite ends of the hall. On 'GO', one person from each team runs to the end of the hall, links arms with one of their team members and together they run back, to link arms with another team member, and so on. If the link is lost, all have to return to the start position and try again, so everybody needs to be considerate of the slowest member's pace and work together.

Reflect together on what you have learnt from this activity.

Islands game 👪

Place large sheets of newspaper on the floor and put the participants in groups. Everyone dances around to music, and when it stops they stand on paper, helping each other not to fall off. Each time, paper is taken away so more have to cooperate to stay on paper. If anyone steps off, then that whole group is out.

Ask how it felt to be left out of the game? How do we leave other people out of our **Fellowship**?

Koinonia or fellowship bracelets 👪 ☺

There are several designs for these, including a simple three-string plait and other more complex designs. Try searching the web for 'friendship bracelet patterns' or 'simple friendship bracelet patterns'.

As people are making the bracelets, discuss with them how the different threads weaving together make something that is beautiful – **Fellowship** works when all of the people work well together, like the threads within a friendship bracelet. They could make them and give them to people with whom they are in **Fellowship**.

For younger children, you could perhaps distribute pre-made bracelets and read a story such as *The Selfish Giant*, considering how the characters were only happy when they accepted each other and lived together peacefully, or *The Enormous Turnip*, where the characters only achieved their goal by working together – explaining that the bracelets are to help them to remember that message.

Encourage one another 👪 ☺

Give each person a small piece of paper and ask them to write their name at the top of the paper and place it in a central box, basket or bag. Each person picks out a name at random from the box and writes words of encouragement for the named person on to the paper. It is then returned to the person by handing it back to them, or anonymously by returning it to the central box for the person to collect.

In the coming week, pray each day for the person you have encouraged in order to deepen your **Fellowship** with one another.

Accept one another 👪 ☺

Have a very large piece of paper, or a number of smaller pieces, and draw a sketch of each person in the group with their name clearly displayed (stick figures are fine!). These can be stuck on the wall or laid out on the floor.

Invite each person to add words or comments to each of the drawings. These words should be positive words or statements about what they admire about that person, what they think is great about the person's personality or character, things that they want to say 'thank you' to them for, what they bring to the group, and so on.

By the end of the exercise, there should be positive comments around each person's drawing showing that they are loved, accepted and valued for who they are within the group.

Allow people time to read all the positive comments. You may choose to display these on the wall afterwards, or use them as a focus for prayers of thanks.

Drama 👪

Divide the group into two and invite one group to create a sketch that shows people being in **Fellowship**, encouraging them to show what it is that creates the **Fellowship**. Ask the other group to create a sketch that shows **Fellowship** falling apart, showing what has caused that. Then ask each group to perform their sketch to the other group. The sketches can be funny or serious.

To make it more fun, you could pick a number of random props and challenge the groups to include the props somehow within their sketches.

Encouraging the groups to explore some verses about **Fellowship** from the Bible before they start creating their sketches may help. For a list to get you started, see the list of verses at the top of p. 24.

FORMING THE HABIT

The ideas presented in this section are offered to help you establish or further practise **Fellowship** as a regular habit personally, as a church and in engagement with your local community and the wider world. You may want to consider using the ideas in more than one of these contexts.

In developing **Fellowship** as a regular habit, you may find some of the material in the 'Understanding the habit' section helpful too.

STORIES TO SHOW THE HABIT FORMING

How could you use these formative and transformative stories to inspire others? What stories of your own could you share?

People of all ages can crave **Fellowship**. This is especially true of young people, who need communities of belonging. Andrew Roberts, in his book *Holy Habits* (Malcolm Down Publishing, 2016), tells of the **Fellowship** that he enjoyed as a young person:

> I was blessed as a young person to grow up in a church community that valued younger people. Amongst many in the church who cared for us, loved us and put up with us in our formative years were Alun and Rose. Their commitment was astonishing. Every Sunday evening, they opened their homes to us and when numbers grew so much that we couldn't fit in, they extended their home. We were welcomed, we were loved, we were listened to. We were served cakes that would put Mary Berry to shame (Rose was the most wonderful cook). We had our hearts repaired when teenage love fell apart. And we were encouraged in our discipleship; taken to evangelistic events where the call of Jesus was clearly presented, encouraged to join in with all sorts of acts of service in the community and given opportunities to explore particular calls and forms of ministry.

Fellowship can form around particular interests and activities within the life of the church. Done well, these **Fellowship** groups can be highly effective witnesses and ways of both presenting Christ and drawing others to him:

> In the first episode of his 2016 BBC series, *Best in Britain*, Gareth Malone featured two choirs that were models of open, welcoming, supportive fellowship. One was Sutton Hill community choir, set in a very needy suburb of Telford. The choir is led by mum-of-three Rachel and the local Anglican vicar, Linda. It has brought people together and stands as a beacon of dignity, purpose and hope in an area of particularly problematic relationships and needs.

The other was the Emmanu'-El Apostolic Gospel Academy, a Pentecostal choir from Leicester, made up of people from countries all over the world including Jamaica, Zimbabwe, Kenya, Nigeria, Bermuda, Canada, Ghana and the UK. United in music and faith, their **Fellowship** has brought joy to the wider community and has been a sign to the city of how people of all nations can live together.

For more on these choirs, search the BBC website for 'The choir: Gareth's best in Britain'.

At Great Barr Methodist Church, **Fellowship** has grown at a Messy Church:

The women who bring their children to Messy Church really value the time spent together chatting over the meal at the end of our sessions. One of the mums expressed a desire to know more about the Bible stories that were explored and so 'Messy Women' was born. We now meet about once every 6–8 weeks in a local pub. As we gather, we share the joys and challenges of life over a drink and often as we **Eat Together**. We explore a Bible passage, topical issue or Holy Habit and we often **Pray** together. But what keeps us coming, and what makes us find space in our busy diaries, is the **Fellowship** that we share as we get to know one another more intimately, as we welcome newcomers, as we support one another through the ups and downs of life and as we explore together as fellow disciples what it means to be Christians in daily life at work, at home and at play.

PRACTICES TO HELP FORM THE HABIT

Here are some suggestions for how **Fellowship** can be part of a rhythm or rule of life in our personal discipleship and in and through the **Fellowship** of our churches.

Often (daily or weekly)

Journalling

Journalling is regularly reflecting on your experiences, thoughts and encounters with God and keeping a note of your reflections. See the Holy Habits Introductory Guide for more information.

As you try to develop the Holy Habit of **Fellowship**, note down in your journal times when you have met together in **Fellowship** and how it made you feel.

Write about when you have noticed times of particularly strong **Fellowship**. Reflect upon what may have made it stronger.

Note what you have found difficult or challenging about being in **Fellowship**. What might God be saying to you about this?

Get to know your neighbours!

Fellowship is all about sharing, caring and living out our faith in actions. In an age where friend counts on Facebook get ever higher, many people long for real, personal meeting and belonging.

How could you, individually or as families, build a sense of belonging with your neighbours? Hosting a barbecue, having a Christmas party, watching the football together (which might bless those who don't like football too if it is only on in one house!). There are endless possibilities.

As a church, how can you be a good neighbour to the communities that surround your meeting place on a weekly basis? How does that inform where you park your cars, the signs on your building, the activities you hold and every aspect of your presence in your community?

Small groups

Small groups have long played a key role in the formation and deepening of **Fellowship**. It is noteworthy that during the New Testament period, churches as a rule were small enough to meet in homes (even if some of the homes were quite large). Ever since, all sorts of groups have been formed and found to be helpful including:

- monastic groups
- cell groups
- home groups
- class meetings
- prayer triplets
- base ecclesial communities.

We could devote an entire booklet to these different forms of group, but will instead simply point out they all testify to the value of meeting in smaller groups. You may wish to review the health of the small groups in your church and explore some different models too.

A good place to start is the small group section of the Methodist Church website (**www.methodist.org.uk/deepening-discipleship/small-groups**).

Build up the fellowship 👪 ☺

Fellowship doesn't just happen! There are many ways to build and strengthen it; a few examples follow.

Send a simple text, tweet or post challenging someone to do something good, or to show how much they care. Make sure *you* also do something good, and show how much *you* care!

To go a little further than this, why not make a small card (the size of a credit card) to encourage someone who is struggling? Give it to them to carry around with them. Spur one another on toward love and good deeds (Hebrews 10:24).

Put on an afternoon tea or similar for a different group in the church from that which you belong to – could the Ladies' Fellowship put on a tea for the youth group, or the Sunday School hold a party for the older members of the congregation, taking into consideration their needs when planning the event?

Set up a prayer station in church where the church family can pray for others. Explain to the church how it is to be used and check it regularly. As a group, pray for the people and situations raised.

Consider which other Holy Habits could build up your **Fellowship**: **Eating Together** and **Prayer** lend themselves easily to this.

Remember that **Fellowship** has many facets and shapes – it can occur in person, online or through a mixture of both.

Get to know each other! As you build **Fellowship**, you may want to learn more about the church projects and non-church activities which others in the fellowship are involved in. Building listening skills will benefit the deepening of **Fellowship** and enable us to welcome and walk alongside people beyond the church community.

Sometimes (weekly or monthly)

Get to know your neighbours!

Do things in the church garden – fêtes, games, music – and be seen to have fun. It's amazing how often people will recognise you as being different, because they have witnessed you working and living out your Christian faith. They then know who to turn to when they need something or someone.

How about hosting a simple lunch and inviting fellow Christians from your local Churches Together group or members of the local community to share **Fellowship**? You may wish to talk with each other about what **Fellowship** means to each of you.

Include the excluded 🛉🛉🛉

Fellowship aims to include, not to exclude. This is an active, not a passive, process – be on the lookout for those who might be excluded from your **Fellowship** – particularly as relationships grow and strengthen. But consider, too, who is excluded in your community – the isolated or housebound, those who are homeless, refugees or asylum seekers, people who are bullied or different in some way. How might you have **Fellowship** with them in a way which challenges their exclusion from society (or a part of it)?

Chaplaincy (e.g. Chaplaincy Everywhere, **www.methodist.org.uk/mission/ chaplaincy/chaplaincy-everywhere**), or Anna Chaplaincy, working specifically with older people, **www.thegiftofyears.org.uk/anna-chaplaincy-older-people**) aims to build **Fellowship** with those who need it, while Parish Nursing (**www.parishnursing. org.uk**) does this as part of whole-person healthcare.

In schools, find out if a buddy scheme operates for playtimes and encourage young people to volunteer. If no such scheme exists for helping children to feel part of the community during break times, then perhaps they can take the challenge to set one up. Playground Buddies (**www.playgroundbuddies.com**) has resources for this.

Extending fellowship ☺

John Wesley was one among others who recognised that God can be encountered in **Fellowship** with those outside the Christian community and on the edges of society. The experience of meeting people we wouldn't normally spend time with can extend our ideas about **Fellowship** and remind us of the radical nature of Christian love.

Consider following Wesley's example and getting involved in a community or social project as an existing fellowship or small group (or talk about the activities you are involved in individually that bring you into contact with people who are different from you).

- What does it feel like to be in an environment where you are a guest?
- How could we extend our **Fellowship** to those we wouldn't naturally come into contact with?
- Where do you see God at work beyond the church?

Occasionally (quarterly, annually)

Review your welcome

Have a training session to develop the welcoming ministry of your church. Could you develop a church welcome pack which could be given to new members and visitors?

Is your **Fellowship** accessible to all? How accessible is it to those with special needs or physical disabilities? Is it dementia aware? How inclusive is it? There is a wealth of resources available about the place and importance of welcome. One good example is *First Impressions Count*, available for free from **www.methodist. org.uk/mission/welcome-and-invitation**. The 'Reach Out' series of books by The Bible Reading Fellowship includes two titles that directly address this area of church communications: *Church from the Inside* and *Church from the Outside*.

Review your fellowship

Challenge yourself to think about your individual **Fellowship** – explore your friendship groups and networks of relationships. Are there relationships you need to invest more in? How could you deepen **Fellowship** in some of these groups?

Survey anonymously how much people feel part of your church fellowship. What has caused those feelings? What do people value about the **Fellowship** they find in church? Don't forget to survey the views of children and young people too.

You might find the following questions helpful:

- What is good about the **Fellowship** you share?
- How might you celebrate these things?
- How does **Fellowship** fall below the *koinonia* that Luke speaks of in Acts 2?
- How could you deepen the experience and expression of **Fellowship**?
- How many people have you welcomed into your **Fellowship** in the past year?
- How might you welcome more?

The 'Everybody Welcome' course by Bob Jackson and George Fisher is described as 'the course where everybody helps grow the church'. It challenges every member of the church to explore what it means to be a welcoming community.

The Grove Booklet *Creating a Culture of Welcome in the Local Church* by Alison Gilchrist contains a 'welcome audit' you might find helpful, with supporting material on the Grove website.

Weekends away and festivals

Youth weekends, church weekends away, pilgrimages and other intentional times for sustained **Fellowship**, learning and **Worship** can be highly formative. They need not be overly expensive, but if resources are really tight then a weekend programme can be based at your local church, with shared meals but people returning to their homes to sleep.

Where resources permit or grants are available, then the Christian festivals typically held at Easter or over the summer are also great opportunities to deepen **Fellowship**, as well as to experience good **Biblical Teaching** and **Worship**. If some might struggle to go to these events, then this is a good place for others to practise **Generosity** or **Sharing Resources**.

9

Fellowship

They devoted themselves to the apostles' teaching and fellowship.
Acts 2:42

I have a theory that the amount we enjoy a wedding is often inversely proportionate to the amount of money spent on it. When I was minister of a church in Edlington, an ex-pit village near Doncaster, we had a fabulous wedding. The bride came from a Tongan family ... an timing. Vi duly arrived forty-five minutes ... tradition of saying goodbye to each ... and was a joyous fusion of ... ultaneously in ... he end

QUESTIONS TO CONSIDER AS A CHURCH

These questions will help your church to consider how it can review the place of **Fellowship** in all of its life together. They are intended to be asked regularly rather than considered once and then forgotten. You will need to determine where in your church the responsibility for each question lies – with the whole church in a general meeting, or with the church leadership, a relevant committee or another grouping. Feel free to add more of your own.

Before exploring the questions, spend some time reflecting on the depth of **Fellowship** that lies within the *koinonia* that Luke presents in Acts 2:42.

Please note that these questions may raise very personal issues. Handle them with prayer and care. Be careful to listen, particularly to the voices of those who may be quieter or less confident. Perceptions of **Fellowship** often vary hugely.

- How does your church reflect and show its **Fellowship** with the divine community of Father, Son and Holy Spirit?
- How deep is the **Fellowship** that you share with each other?
- In what ways is the **Fellowship** that you share similar and dissimilar to the community described in Acts 2?
- Is your **Fellowship** deeper for some than for others? Who might feel excluded?
- How do you include those who are suffering in your **Fellowship**?
- What is the welcome like in your church? Who is involved?
- How important is Matthew 25:35 – 'I was a stranger and you welcomed me' – to your church?
- How are long-term members made to feel as welcome as visitors?

- What more could you do to create and maintain an atmosphere of acceptance and inclusion at your church?
- Is there a strong intergenerational **Fellowship**, i.e. between children, young people, adults and older people?
- How could you practise other Holy Habits to deepen your **Fellowship**?
- How might acts of **Serving** foster **Fellowship**? What might you *do* together?
- What do you, or could you, do to strengthen **Fellowship** with other churches and denominations in your area?
- How can you develop **Fellowship** with the local community?
- How can you support and encourage **Fellowship** within families at home?

CONNECTING THE HABITS

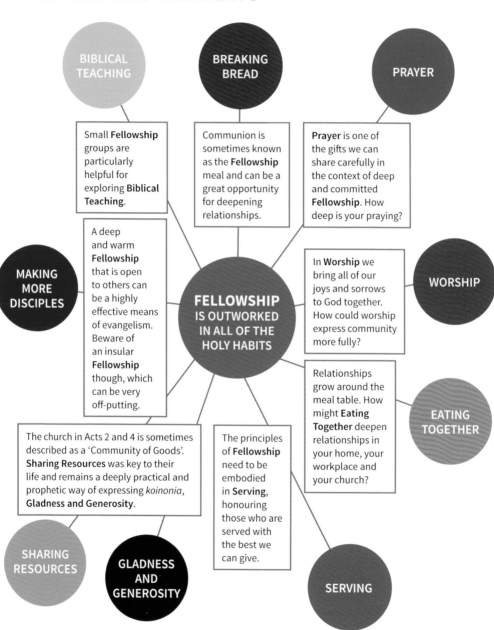

BIBLICAL TEACHING

Small **Fellowship** groups are particularly helpful for exploring **Biblical Teaching**.

BREAKING BREAD

Communion is sometimes known as the **Fellowship** meal and can be a great opportunity for deepening relationships.

PRAYER

Prayer is one of the gifts we can share carefully in the context of deep and committed **Fellowship**. How deep is your praying?

MAKING MORE DISCIPLES

A deep and warm **Fellowship** that is open to others can be a highly effective means of evangelism. Beware of an insular **Fellowship** though, which can be very off-putting.

FELLOWSHIP IS OUTWORKED IN ALL OF THE HOLY HABITS

In **Worship** we bring all of our joys and sorrows to God together. How could worship express community more fully?

WORSHIP

Relationships grow around the meal table. How might **Eating Together** deepen relationships in your home, your workplace and your church?

EATING TOGETHER

The church in Acts 2 and 4 is sometimes described as a 'Community of Goods'. **Sharing Resources** was key to their life and remains a deeply practical and prophetic way of expressing *koinonia*, **Gladness and Generosity**.

The principles of **Fellowship** need to be embodied in **Serving**, honouring those who are served with the best we can give.

SHARING RESOURCES

GLADNESS AND GENEROSITY

SERVING

GOING FURTHER WITH THE HABIT

Depth in fellowship

Biblical **Fellowship** is much deeper than the sometimes-superficial togetherness which the word is often taken to mean in church language – influenced as we have been by the mindset of the modern age. Referring to friendship in order to try to convey something of the deeper meaning of **Fellowship** is only partially effective, given the similar superficialisation of the modern understanding of friendship.

It is worth noting that in his book *The Four Loves*, C.S. Lewis identifies friendship as one of the four kinds of love which were recognised in previous ages, including the biblical era. In the Old Testament, we can see an example of this in the friendship of David and Jonathan. In the New Testament, it is in John 15:12–17 that we find Jesus describing his disciples as friends. Jesus speaks of friendship in terms of love for one another, the kind of love that makes one willing to lay down one's life for one's friends. The Christian concept of friendship is far deeper than Facebook friends!

These verses in John follow directly on from Jesus' teaching that we are related to the Son of God as branches are to the vine. And that means that we are related to each other as branches of the same vine. Here is an insight into the depth of the meaning of **Fellowship** – *koinonia* – in the New Testament. This understanding of the deep, interconnected nature of **Fellowship** is reinforced when we read what Jesus says before the parable of the vine. In John 14:10, Jesus says, 'I am in the Father and the Father is in me', and then in verse 20, 'I am in my Father, and you in me, and I in you'.

There is a mystery here which our minds cannot penetrate fully, although images like the vine and the branches help us to grasp something of it. Paul uses the image of the body to the same purpose, in 1 Corinthians 12:12–27 but also elsewhere. We are members of the body of Christ. Again, this is not simply in the modern sense of membership – the original meaning of 'member' referred to an organ of the body. Paul is saying that we are all organs of one body, Christ's body, 'so we, who are many, are one body in Christ, and individually we are members one of another' (Romans 12:5). Such is the meaning of the **Fellowship** in the example of the earliest Christian church.

Fellowship is not an easy thing to practise consistently as a Christian community. This can be seen in the frequency and the passion with which Paul admonishes the young churches in his letters. Among others, Romans is worth reflecting on, particularly 12:3–13 and 14:1—15:13, but the call to this kind of *koinonia* is a theme which is found frequently in the other New Testament epistles also.

The ideas and resources in this section are offered to help you explore, discover and live more fully the riches and depths of *koinonia* – **Fellowship**.

DEVELOPING FURTHER PRACTICES OF FELLOWSHIP

As you seek to go deeper in your exploration and practice of **Fellowship**, ensure that full and proper safeguarding policies are in place and practices are adhered to. Beware any practices that are manipulative or coercive. If you have any concerns that **Fellowship** might be being abused, speak to your minister or safeguarding officer.

Fellowship and conflict

Fellowship might be comfortable when we are sharing and spending time with people with whom we agree. **Fellowship**, however, can also be uncomfortable. Christians are called to live, work and worship together despite different deeply held views and so demonstrate God's love in the way we engage with each other and the world (John 13:34–35). John Wesley reflects in his sermon 'On a Catholic spirit', 'Though we cannot think alike, may we not love alike? May we not be of one heart, though we are not of one opinion? Without all doubt, we may.'

Christians have found that it is possible to work with people of other denominations or faiths in acts of service or on community projects despite their differences of opinion or beliefs, but history and scripture give ample evidence of various levels of conflict within and between Christian churches – from differences of opinion to more serious division.

The harmony depicted in the Holy Habits passage of Acts 2:42–47 is seen, not much further on in Luke's narrative, to be under severe stress. At the beginning of 1 Corinthians, Paul tells the Christians in Corinth to stop arguing among themselves, to be of one mind and united in thought and purpose.

Fellowship and conflict would appear to be direct opposites. The gospel is a gospel of reconciliation (2 Corinthians 5:17–21), so what should we do when faced with conflict that becomes a source of serious division? The fight/flight alternatives might be familiar, but there are other responses.

There are a number of team-building tools that many churches have found useful in developing their understanding of themselves and others. Bridge Builders (**www. bbministries.org.uk**) is an agency which specifically seeks to 'transform the culture of the church in relation to how leaders lead and the way conflict is handled'. They offer a range of training courses and workshops and lead tailored learning events on request. In addition, they provide coaching, consultancy and mediation services. On the basis that a degree of conflict is inevitable at least from time to time in any Christian fellowship, the expressed aim is to 'strengthen the ministry of Christian leaders, by helping them to be more self-aware, and to develop greater skills, confidence and resilience for working with tensions and conflict in the church'.

The Bridge Builders approach suggests that some experience of conflict is not only inevitable but can also be positive. In developing an awareness of our own response to conflict, we can find ways not only to resolve it but potentially to transform it. Whether our natural response would be to force a situation to get our own way, to look for compromise, to collaborate with others to find a shared view, to accommodate another's position at the cost of our own, or to avoid conflict altogether, it is through our self-understanding and our understanding of others that we develop ways to live through such situations without the more serious and destructive consequences of conflict.

Colin Patterson, Assistant Director of Bridge Builders, suggests six options for responding to a difference over an important issue which might threaten to split the fellowship. Four of these – prayer, giving responsibility to the leaders, leaving, demanding resignations – are common, yet they each have their problems as they leave the responsibility somewhere else. Conflict might only be transformed if all engage in the process. Recognising your own role and seeking a way forward together is vital. So, two less common responses are suggested which can be positive and constructive. Firstly, we recognise our call to be peacemakers – that means developing good listening, which is not always easy, but is essential if conflict is to be transformed. The final option is to suggest that an outsider, who can be more objective and unpick some of the complexity that is usual in any conflict, might help.

Bridge Builders also emphasise the importance of being prepared. It is difficult to make a considered and careful response when the temperature is raised and feelings run high. It is better to have considered these issues in the cold light of day – before the serious situation and the potential for destructive division develop rather than in their midst.

Some questions to ponder

- Think of a situation of conflict you have known or experienced. What were the causes? What were the consequences? How was the situation resolved? In what ways did the conflict result in transformation?
- How do you/might you demonstrate the gospel of reconciliation in the church and in the community? What are the needs that you might respond to?
- What are the strengths of your **Fellowship**? What are the weaknesses? How well do people know one another? Where are the barriers? Are there broken relationships? Where do bridges need to be built?
- Are there sticking-points or no-go areas that you are aware of in the life of your **Fellowship**? How do you encourage honesty and integrity while 'maintain[ing] the unity of the Spirit in the bonds of peace' (Ephesians 4:3)?
- How does the church approach vulnerability and risk? How might potential and actual situations of conflict be addressed positively and creatively to build up and strengthen the **Fellowship**?

Fellowship in suffering

> I want to know Christ and the power of his resurrection and the sharing of his sufferings by becoming like him in his death.
> PHILIPPIANS 3:10

Where the NRSV speaks of 'the sharing of his sufferings', the King James Version refers to 'the fellowship of his sufferings', translating *koinonia* in the original Greek. There is something mysterious in this phrase, the *koinonia* of Christ's sufferings. This is underlined when we read Colossians 1:24, where Paul says, 'I am now rejoicing in my sufferings for your sake, and in my flesh I am completing what is lacking in Christ's afflictions for the sake of his body, that is, the church.' If we think of Christ's suffering only in terms of 'theories of the Atonement', which focus on Jesus paying the price for our sins, we may miss other perspectives which Paul brings to us here in these verses from the letters to the Philippians and the Colossians.

Paul is suffering imprisonment and facing possible execution as he writes about sharing Christ's sufferings in his letter to the church at Philippi. Christians who are experiencing pain, trouble or sorrow have often taken comfort from the knowledge that Jesus also suffered and is in solidarity with our human experience. Suffering is part of life. Christians have also suffered for their faith and continue to do so. Paul says that our suffering connects us with Christ's suffering. However, this doesn't mean that suffering is something God wants for people or something to seek out.

There is more, though, to the solidarity of Christ with human experience than simply empathy at a distance. To Paul, Christ is not just an individual person, just as Adam is not just an individual person. We who are 'in Adam' have been called to be 'in Christ' (see 1 Corinthians 15:22). Paul speaks repeatedly in his letters of being 'in Christ', and he says that those who are in Christ constitute Christ's body. We have *koinonia* with Christ and with all who are in Christ. We share in the *koinonia*/**Fellowship** of the Son of God, which the Son also has with the Father (1 John 1:3).

Given the nature of this world, that **Fellowship** is a fellowship of suffering. Christ comes to a world marked by terrible, wasteful suffering. He himself submits to suffering, and his suffering becomes the means by which many are made righteous (Isaiah 53:11). Suffering becomes the means of redemption. Commentaries differ on how to interpret Paul's statement that his suffering helps 'complete' or 'fill up' the suffering of Christ, but perhaps we can take it that as we are members of Christ's body, our sufferings too are not wasteful but somehow take on meaning and purpose as we participate in the 'fellowship of his suffering'. It is also a **Fellowship** we are called to share with one another as members of his body.

Like Paul, those who suffer can have spiritual insights that are missed by those who are always active and in control.

- How could we listen to the voices of those in our churches and communities who are subject to the will of others, including children, those who are housebound, people with chronic illnesses, asylum seekers and refugees? How can we hear their opinions, spiritual needs and insights?
- Consider sharing in suffering by voluntarily relinquishing control of an event or a role to others. How could those who are often passive be given a chance to do and serve?

For more on suffering as being subject to the actions of others, read William Vanstone's short book *The Stature of Waiting* (Morehouse Publishing, 2006).

Chaplaincy

Chaplaincy can be particularly effective in inspiring **Fellowship**. One minister shares his experiences of informal chaplaincy 'on the hill' (names have been changed):

One event sticks in the mind. It was 6.15 am on a Sunday morning, and very cold. I don't know who was more reluctant to be on the hill, me or my dog, but I was preaching later in the day and this was the only chance for a walk. The freezing mist was parted first by a familiar Staffie, and then a mildly disembodied voice that hailed me with 'Hey, I want a word!'

Anne, who had now appeared out of the mist, was a regular dog walker on our field, and often chatted; today, she was troubled. I can remember sharing a beautiful sunset with her one evening, with very few words needed, and she had been with me when another regular came without Ted, her elderly Westie, who had been put down that morning: I never knew this lady's name, only that of her dog.

Being chaplain, whether to soldiers, patients or dog walkers, means sharing in the life of others. That might be deep conversation or silent tears, glorious sunshine or battling the rain. You share in what everyone else gets, and become a catalyst for others to share too. Like when 'the Colonel' joined us. We called him that because of his upright manner and 'tache, but we never learned his name. He walked slowly, with a stick, but rarely spoke. He wanted to be with us even though he didn't have a dog. Alone in retirement, he joined the **Fellowship**; we opened up to share our company with him.

Chaplaincy helps transform a community to care for itself, and to care for others. It's an excuse for people to accept and care for each other. It's an example of how they can love.

The Colonel was always welcome, Ted's mum kept coming, and when new arrival Margaret's husband died, they were there for her.

More information on chaplaincy, including the Chaplaincy Everywhere course, can be found on the Methodist Chaplaincy website: **www.methodist.org.uk/mission/chaplaincy**. Other denominations will have other resources too.

Covenant and fellowship

The Covenant Service introduced by John Wesley is a gift that many different churches have come to value, using elements of it as a way of expressing their discipleship and affirming their **Fellowship** with God, with one another and with the world. In the introduction to the Covenant Service in *The Methodist Worship Book*, we find these words:

> The covenant is not just a one-to-one transaction between individuals and God, but the act of the whole faith community. The prayers of intercession which follow [the Covenant prayer] emphasise our unity with all humanity.
> *The Methodist Worship Book* (1999), pp. 281–82

The theology of Covenant is a theology of **Fellowship** – deep commitment, based on:

- the mutual commitment we see within the divine community of Father and Son and Holy Spirit and the commitment of that community to humanity
- the response of the people of God to that divine commitment
- the commitment of the people of God to one another and to the world.

Have a look at the Methodist Covenant Service and think how this could be for you more fully an act of *koinonia* – **Fellowship**.

Sharing your story

It's easy to experience **Fellowship** in a place where we feel like we fit in.

Can you think of a time when you have been welcomed into the **Fellowship** of a group where you might not have naturally used the 'churchy' word **Fellowship**; where you have had a real sense of at-oneness with those around you and a sense of the presence of God in the midst of a secular setting?

What does it tell you about what it means to be in **Fellowship** with God?

What does this experience have to teach you about **Fellowship** within a Christian context?

How could this story shape your faith story and that of your church and community?

How could you share it with others?

ARTS AND MEDIA

There are many films and books containing scenes about **Fellowship** which could be used as an illustration in worship. However, it is suggested that the following films and books are watched or read in their entirety and followed by a discussion to go deeper into the topic of **Fellowship**.

Films

Harry Potter and the Philosopher's Stone (PG, 2011, 2h32m)

The Harry Potter novels and films chronicle the life of a young wizard, Harry Potter, and his friends. **Fellowship** is at the heart of Harry's journey through the whole series of films as he faces all sorts of unforeseen dangers and situations. The first film, based on the book of the same name, introduces the main players and the events which first build their **Fellowship**.

- Harry enters a new world, a world about which he knew nothing until he heard from Hogwarts. How does Harry's experience of joining the magical community as a relatively uninformed outsider challenge our understanding of being 'in' or 'out' of the **Fellowship** of the church?
- Who are the 'muggles' in our communities? How do we practise **Fellowship** with them?

The Help (12A, 2011, 2h26m)

Set in the American south in the 1960s, a southern society girl is determined to be a writer. She chooses to write about the local black women who are the hired help for the white families, a potentially dangerous book to write during the turbulent era of segregation. Based on the book of the same name, this is a story of courage and friendship, of divisions and strengths within communities.

- Where do you see the most powerful displays of friendship and **Fellowship** in this film?
- What are the values that underpin the different communities in the film, and the **Fellowship** that exists as a result?
- What might be a similarly risky subject to write about in your context today? What does this say about who might be excluded from **Fellowship**?

🏃 The Lion King (U, 1994, 1h29m)

A film that captures divisions in family and community that lead to a time away from home. Ultimately, there is reconciliation and restoration into community.

- Where and how does Simba find **Fellowship** when he flees his community?
- What responsibility do we have to remain in **Fellowship** with those among whom God has 'cast our lot'?

The Lord of the Rings: The Fellowship of the Ring
(PG, 2001, 2h58m)

When a long-lost ring of dark power resurfaces, an extraordinary group of individuals must come together to embark on a mission that will forge bonds of **Fellowship** that will overcome the harshest of challenges and save Middle Earth. Based on the book of the same name, this first film of three culminates in the gathering of the **Fellowship**, each member pledging what they bring with them to the common cause.

- What could the way that the **Fellowship** forms around a quest tell us about how **Fellowship** might form around mission?
- The different members of the **Fellowship** of the ring all come together for different reasons, with different motivations and with different gifts – but with a single purpose. Explore how these themes might help you grow deeper **Fellowship** in your church or small group.

🏃 Over the Hedge (U, 2006, 1h23m)

A group of animals work together to store food for the winter. See what happens when another animal joins the team.

- How does the animal community in the film embody **Fellowship**?
- What can the film teach us about how to respond when someone new arrives and shakes up our expression of **Fellowship**?

🏃 Paddington (PG, 2014, 1h35m)

A young bear from Peru travels to London and is in need of a home. He is taken in by the kindly Brown family, who found him at Paddington station. He soon becomes very much part of their family, despite the many incidents that he gets involved in. Based on a series of books.

- Strong **Fellowship** develops within the Brown family over the course of the film. What causes this and what changes occur?
- What challenge can a story like this bring to your family, or to the church?

👪 Toy Story (PG, 1995, 1h21m)

In this classic animated film, the **Fellowship** among Andy's toys is shaken up and changed for ever by the arrival of new toy, Buzz Lightyear. While cowboy Woody is initially extremely hostile to the new arrival, a shared quest builds lasting **Fellowship** among the toys.

- How is your church's **Fellowship** changed by the arrival of new people?
- How can you build acceptance and resilience into your **Fellowship**?
- What is your uniting quest and how are you tackling it?

Books: fiction

Are there people in your church or local community who would like to discuss some of these books at a book club? Guidance on how to form these is widely available online, and you could also ask denominational training officers for help.

The Beach House
Sally John (Harvest House Publishers, 2006)

The story of four friends who meet to celebrate their 40th birthdays together. They reminisce about their shared histories and share their varied experiences. Will the problems of the past threaten their present? As they share together, their universal desire for understanding, identity, faith and friendship is the bond which binds the four friends together in this endearing story.

- How can a shared past positively shape the future?

Charlotte Gray
Sebastian Faulks
(Random House, 1999)

Charlotte Gray is a young Scottish woman who goes to occupied France in 1942 to run a simple errand for a British special operations group, and ends up being drawn into an extraordinary **Fellowship** of resistance fighters and assimilated French Jews, forging lasting bonds amidst the worst of humanity.

- How have difficult situations been formative of **Fellowship** for you?

👪 Chocolate Mousse for Greedy Goose
Julia Donaldson, Nick Sharratt
(Pan Macmillan, 2009)

This simple rhyming tale explores the joys and challenges of **Eating Together** and sharing **Fellowship**.

- What can we learn from this book about sharing life together?

Gangsta Granny
David Walliams (Harper Collins, 2011)

This hilarious story tells of a developing relationship between Ben and his Gran.

- How does this story help us to understand **Fellowship**?
- If we spend time with others, perhaps those we might not choose to, how can **Fellowship** develop?

The Hobbit
J.R.R. Tolkien (George Allen & Unwin, 1937)

An innocent and home-loving hobbit finds himself on a quest to steal gold from Smaug, the dragon, with a motley band of dwarves. Despite initial hostility, a strong **Fellowship** develops between the band of thieves which changes all of them. Adapted into a trilogy of films.

- What can we learn from this classic story about forming community?

Sisterchicks in Wooden Shoes
(and other novels in the series)
Robin Jones Gunn (Waterbrook Multnomah, 2009)

Sisterchick: a friend who shares the deepest wonders of your heart, loves you like a sister and provides you with a reality check. *Sisterchicks in Wooden Shoes* is a reminder of what a blessed gift true and lasting friendship is, a heart-warming tale of two women whose lives are woven together with the golden thread of friendship. The special bond these Sisterchicks share resonates in our souls as they bestow God's blessings on one another in the midst of life's difficult circumstances.

- Does this book offer a model for deep **Fellowship**?

Winnie the Pooh
A.A. Milne (Methuen & Co, 1926)

Classic children's tales of diverse characters living out **Fellowship**, friendship and community despite their differences, and with profound insight into life too.

- How is **Fellowship** expressed by this diverse community?
- How do similarity and difference enrich or conflict with **Fellowship**?

Books: non-fiction

Creating a Culture of Welcome in the Local Church (Grove Evangelism 66)
Alison Gilchrist (Grove Books, 2004)

A brief but helpful overview of the importance of welcome, to help others share true **Fellowship**.

- Might your church need to refresh its culture of welcome?

The Grace Outpouring: Becoming a people of blessing
Roy Godwin and Dave Roberts (David C. Cook, 2012)

Roy and his wife Daphne Godwin have been at Ffaldy-Brenin Retreat Centre near the Pembrokeshire coast of Wales for almost ten years. In that time, they have seen God's power break through into the lives of visitors from all over the world.

This terrific book recounts some of these stories of the power of God's love and grace changing people's lives in amazing ways.

- What is the relationship between **Fellowship**, mission and evangelism?

The Hiding Place
Corrie ten Boom, with John and Elizabeth Sherrill (Hodder & Stoughton, 1971)

Corrie ten Boom's astonishing biography tells of how her family extended **Fellowship** to persecuted Jews during the Nazi occupation of Holland, and how this led to them building **Fellowship** in the horrific concentration camp, Ravensbrück – and even, through forgiveness, offering **Fellowship** to those who had persecuted them there.

- To whom could your **Fellowship** be opened to offer welcome and safety?

Koinonia: A recipe for authentic fellowship
Charles R. Swindoll (Insight for Living, 1995)

A Bible study guide comprising a series of reflections on love, humility, restoration, forgiveness and encouragement that can be used for personal reflection or by a Bible study group.

- Could you use this, or develop your own series, to study the biblical understanding of *koinonia* further?

Miracle on the River Kwai (also known as **Through the Valley of the Kwai**)
Ernest Gordon (Harper, 1962)

Ernest Gordon's autobiography tells of his experiences of **Fellowship** in a Japanese prisoner of war labour camp, building the Burma railway during World War II. Adapted into a film: *To End All Wars* (15, 2001, 2h5m).

- What does this book teach us about the **Fellowship** of suffering?

A New Monastic Handbook: From vision to practice
Ian Mobsby and Mark Berry (Canterbury Press Norwich, 2013)

A very helpful book, both theologically and practically, full of insights into how new monasticism can form or renew missional **Fellowship**.

- What insights might new monasticism offer to the **Fellowship** groups that you are part of, or are seeking to form?

Practising Community: The task of the local church
Robin Greenwood (SPCK, 1996)

An excellent reflection on how the New Testament concept of *koinonia* should deeply influence the way that we live out Christian community in the church.

- How might you extend the principles in this book to live out the values of *koinonia* in the day-to-day life of the world as well?

Articles and online media

Exploring Spiritual Practices

Session 6 of the Methodist Church's series Exploring Spiritual Practices (**www.methodist.org.uk/deepening-discipleship/spiritual-practices/exploring-spiritual-practices**) explores **Fellowship**.

Good News Stories

Redditch Community Centre (**youtu.be/cGzJqiEqbvQ** or search YouTube for 'Good News Stories with Nick').

It's cold: join a small group

The Skit Guys perform a short sketch, which points out that we are in an age of social isolation, and **Fellowship** is very important (**youtu.be/QpfBTG0nyvA** or search YouTube for 'It's cold: join a small group').

Music

The following songs may help you to explore and reflect further on this habit.

One Love
Bob Marley

A powerful cry for people to come together under the love of the Father of creation. A rich blend of **Worship**, lament and **Fellowship**.

We All Stand Together (The Frog Chorus)
Paul McCartney

(What's so funny 'bout) Peace, Love and Understanding
Elvis Costello

A song that affirms and celebrates the power of peace, love and understanding to bring people together in times of darkness and danger.

Stained Glass Masquerade
Casting Crowns

A song which questions the
superficiality of our **Fellowship**.

Poetry

A number of poems are presented or referenced below. Choose one to reflect on.

You may wish to consider some of the following questions:

- What does this poem say to you about **Fellowship**?
- Which images do you find helpful or unhelpful?
- How is your practice of **Fellowship** challenged by this poem?
- Could you write a poem to share with others the virtues of **Fellowship**?

Together (celebrating **Fellowship**)

Walk with me, and I with you.
Journeying together we give of ourselves.
We risk as we share:
my traditions laid bare by your 'why?'.
Opening my soul I risk your scorn, pity, anger.
Your counter perspective widens my view
of self and of life.
We do not agree on everything,
yet find we are no longer afraid to differ.
Actively choosing contrasting experiences,
we come together to tell our stories.
Trusting you with my deepest thoughts,
I hold yours as a precious gift
rare and fragile.

Intangible, unfathomable, priceless.
What we share defies description.
Slipping between the lines
of definition, is this an illusion?
Take my hand again.
Journeying together we give of ourselves,
I walk with you, and you with me.

Tricia Mitchell

Bread and Roses
from the film *Pride*, available on YouTube (**youtu.be/qNQs6gSOkeU** or search YouTube for 'Bread and Roses')

The Lighthouse Keepers
Ian Adams from *Cave Refectory Road* (Canterbury Press, 2010)

Light a Candle (To Start a Fire)
Ian Adams from *Running Over Rocks* (Canterbury Press, 2013)

Sacramental
Pádraig Ó Tuama from *Sorry For Your Troubles* (Canterbury Press, 2013)

Visual

The Supper at Emmaus

Ceri Richards (1903–71): gouache, 1958, 40 x 40 cm.

From the Methodist Modern Art Collection, © TMCP, used with permission.

You can download this image from: www.methodist.org.uk/artcollection

In creating the Methodist Modern Art Collection, Douglas Wollen had admired Ceri Richards' altarpiece in the chapel at St Edmund Hall, Oxford, and had contacted the artist about the possibility of a further commission. The artist replied that he had 'a small gouache study of the St Edmund Hall *Supper at Emmaus*' – it was this study which was added to the Methodist Collection around 1962.

It depicts the story in Luke 24 where two travellers invite a stranger on the road to sup with them at Emmaus. 'When he was at the table with them, he took bread, gave thanks, broke it and began to give it to them. Then their eyes were opened, and they recognised him.'

- Notice how the artist uses colour to convey the moment of epiphany. The shady slatted shape at the top left, suggestive of a closed window, is echoed in the black horizontal bars of the chair. The chair is rocked off balance as the dark-haired figure recognises Jesus, leaning towards his companion out of fear or for moral support. It seems that the figure in green has already reached a place of recognition, hands clasped in adoration. Is it reading too much into the palette to suggest that if the golden figure infuses or illuminates the figure in blue, then this disciple will become as his fellow in green, Christ in him, renewed in hope?
- As we follow the gaze of the figure in green, our eye goes to the head of Jesus and then to the pointed white jug, strategically positioned on the cross piece, which is also the table. What does this say to you about divine **Fellowship**?
- Draw or paint something that evokes the depth and breadth of **Fellowship** you have experienced.

Relaxed fellowship

Explore the setting of this photograph – particularly what you might think of as usual or expected and what is unexpected or unusual – and how the sharing of **Fellowship** might be understood and experienced in and through the life of your church and community.

- What do you think are the essential features of **Fellowship**?
- Where do you see those features in this photograph?

Credits

In addition to the Holy Habits editorial/development team, contributions to this booklet also came from: Vicki Atkinson, Andrew Brazier, Keith Dennis, Brian Dickens, Jacky Goaten, Dorothy Graham, Gill Holmes, Nick Jones, Alison Mares, Sarah Middleton, Tom Milton, Tricia Mitchell, Joan Pulley, Linda Ramdharry, Claire Rawlinson, Marjorie Roper, David Rosser and Diane Webb.

'This set of ten resources will enable churches and individuals to begin to establish "habits of faithfulness". In the United Reformed Church, we are calling this process of developing discipleship, "Walking the Way: Living the life of Jesus today" and I have no doubt that this comprehensive set of resources will enable us to do just that.'
Revd Richard Church, Deputy General Secretary (Discipleship), United Reformed Church

'Here are some varied and rich resources to help further deepen our discipleship of Christ, encouraging and enabling us to adopt the life-transforming habits that make for following Jesus.'
Revd Dr Martyn Atkins, Team Leader & Superintendent Minister, Methodist Central Hall, Westminster

'The Holy Habits resources will help you, your church, your fellowship group, to engage in a journey of discovery about what it really means to be a disciple today. I know you will be encouraged, challenged and inspired as you read and work your way through each chapter. There is lots to study together and pray about, and that can only be good as our churches today seek to bring about the kingdom of God.'
Revd Loraine Mellor, President of the Methodist Conference 2017/18

'The Holy Habits resources help weave the spiritual through everyday life. They're a great tool that just get better with use. They help us grow in our desire to follow Jesus as their concern is formation not simply information.'
Olive Fleming Drane and John Drane

'The Holy Habits resources are an insightful and comprehensive manual for living in the way of Jesus in the 21st century: an imaginative, faithful and practical gift for the church that will sustain and invigorate our life and mission in a demanding world. The Holy Habits resources are potentially transformational for a church.'
Revd Ian Adams, Mission Spirituality Adviser for Church Mission Society

'To understand the disciplines of the Christian life without practising them habitually is like owning a fine collection of soap but never having a wash. The team behind Holy Habits knows this, which is why they have produced these excellent and practical resources. Use them, and by God's grace you will grow in holiness.'
Paul Bayes, Bishop of Liverpool

'The Holy Habits resources are a rich mine of activities for all ages to help change minds, attitudes and behaviours. I love the way many different people groups are represented and celebrated, and the constant references to the complex realities of 21st-century life.'
Lucy Moore, Founder of BRF's Messy Church